THE CHARITY EVENT PLANNING GUIDE

$14.95

THE CHARITY EVENT PLANNING GUIDE
Having Fun While Raising Funds

David Mirisch and Godfrey Harris

THE AMERICAS GROUP
520 S. Selpulveda Blvd., Suite 204
Los Angeles, CA 90049 USA

FIRST EDITION   1st Printing — September 2012
2nd Printing — November 2012

The Americas Group
520 S. Sepulveda Blvd., Suite 204
Los Angeles, California 90049-3534
U.S.A

☎   + (1) 310 476 6374
FX   + (1) 310 471 3276
EM   hrmg@mac.com
WWW   AMERICASGROUP.COM

ISBN:
978-0-935047-75-2

Library of Congress Cataloging-in-Publication Data

Mirisch, David, 1935-
  The charity event planning guide : having fun while raising funds / David Mirisch and Godfrey Harris. -- 1st ed.
      p. cm.
  Includes bibliographical references and index.
  ISBN 978-0-935047-75-2 (alk. paper)
  1. Fund raising. 2. Charities. I. Harris, Godfrey, 1937- II. Title.
  HV41.2.M57 2012
  658.15'224--dc23
                              2012032927

CONTENTS OF THE CHARITY EVENT PLANNING GUIDE

DEDICATED TO

everyone generous enough
to take the time
and make the effort
to plan the details
that make charitable events both
meaningful and memorable.

David Mirisch
Missoula, Montana
August 2012

Godfrey Harris
Los Angeles, California
August 2012

THOUGHTS ON CHARITY EVENTS
An Introduction by David Mirisch

Ronald McDonald House at Stanford

Bulan Sabit Merah Malaysia

DOING THE MOST GOOD™

BOY SCOUTS OF AMERICA®

MAKE·(A)·WISH.

Until Every One Comes Home.®

American Heart Association | American Stroke Association.

Logos of some of the charitable organizations that David Mirisch Enterprises has worked with over the years.

DAVID MIRISCH ON THE PRINCIPLES OF ORGANIZING A SUCCESSFUL CHARITY EVENT

During my 40 years working with nonprofit organizations, family members, friends, and business associates have often told me that others could benefit from what I have done in a career that has involved raising more than $35,000,000. After talking with Godfrey Harris, someone I have known from my school days in Los Angeles, we decided to co-write this Guide to fund raising events for nonprofit groups because we wanted a document that could benefit every organization of every size. I have had the honor of helping establish two of the now biggest nonprofits in the United States — The Make-A-Wish Foundation of Los Angeles and the Pancreatic Cancer Action Network — and some of the smallest as well. It is that background along with Godfrey's planning experience in government and business that informs the ideas in this book.

Every week, it seems, I have met with some kind of nonprofit that needs help. The first question I ask them is a very simple one: "Do you need to raise money?" If they do, we then go through elements found in this Guide — step-by-step and document by document — with me explaining how to respond to every question and approach every option.

The people I work with soon realize that it takes *teamwork* to raise real money for a charitable group through a successful event. There are two basic needs to accomplish this:

- A good CHAIRPERSON — dedicated, committed, and energetic — is the key to a memorable event that leads to a bigger bank account.

- A good STEERING COMMITTEE of at least ten people. Even when I have met with very small nonprofits — groups who claim that they have only 3 or 4 people that can really be counted on to help with organizational needs — I insist that they find ten for a steering committee.

With Pat Boone

With wife Sandy, Barron Hilton

With Arnold Schwarzenegger

With Shaquille O'Neal

With Lawrence Welk

With Bill Walton in photo

With Julie Andrews

With Frank Sinatra

Photos of some of the celebrities that David Mirisch has involved in the events he has planned and coordinated.

Let's look at these two fundamental needs more closely. In the world of fund raising, we use the term "leader" — the person who guides the event from start to finish. He or she is the person who actually "runs" every aspect of an event — the boss, chief, manager, coach, or honcho in other settings. In Hollywood, the person in charge of a reality TV show or an on-going series is actually referred to as the "runner." Event leaders bring expertise, knowledge, and understanding to the task at hand. The leader can be a consultant, the organization's chairperson, or one of its paid staff. The leader sees that the steering committee is doing all of the things it is supposed to do and works hand in hand with subcommittee heads to insure that their groups are accomplishing their assigned tasks. Nothing is "set in stone" by a subcommittee without final approval of the event leader. And, nothing is ever spent without the approval of either the event leader or the person responsible for the nonprofit organization itself.

The bigger the steering committees for an event, the better the event is likely to be. I view ten as the *minimum* number needed for a successful event. Those 10, by the way, do *not* include staff people who are generally occupied with their normal duties and ought not to be diverted to the management of a special event. Inevitably, a few people drop off of a steering committee for various reasons as the date for the event draws closer. When people leave a steering committee, their work assignments usually devolve on the leader or the staff if there are insufficient committee members to take up the slack. The lack of manpower usually means something important gets left out. For a number of years I did a golf tournament for the Simi Valley Kiwanis Club in California. They had 25 people on their steering committee. They met for dinner every other week at a different committee member's home. The result was a wonderful event, year in and year out. My experience tells me that if you cannot get a minimum of eight people for a steering committee, your event will likely fall well short of its goals. A lot of work will be done for very little effect. There is strength in numbers. Get them before you begin.

I have often been asked about the best way to appeal to someone to lead an event, serve on a steering committee, or simply volunteer for whatever jobs need doing. I always remind people that "charity begins at home." And, it really does. Of the 2,500 events that I have planned, managed or consulted on over the years, the most successful ones have been those where leaders, steering committee members, and volunteers really "care" for a cause and have a *feel* for it. They *want* to help. I do an annual WALK each year in Orange County, California, for FSH (a form of muscular dystrophy.) Our best volunteers are those who have FSH or have a friend or relative who has FSH. They *care* about raising the money to help someone suffering from the disease.

Many times an explanation of the cause will 'turn the tide" and produce a battalion of willing workers. Have them look at videos or go to the charity's website for inspiration; send them inside information. People *will* turn on to a cause once educated by someone passionate about it. Once they learn, "they will come." Take the Pancreatic Cancer Action Network. It began when family members of two wonderful ladies in Los Angeles were diagnosed with the disease. Pamela Marquardt and Stephanie Davis wanted to help. They gathered 20 of their friends who were touched by this disease and called a meeting in Century City. The first gala at The Beverly Hills Hotel drew 250 people. The next year we were at the Beverly Hilton and 500 people came to the gala. By the third year we were at the Universal Hilton and 1,000 people attended. Today, the Pancreatic Cancer Action Network has chapters all over the world. And it started because just *two* people cared enough to do something.

Should an effort be made to include "celebrities" in an event? My answer is always "*yes, if the fit is right.*" We have involved some kind of celebrity — movie and television stars, singers and entertainers, local and world class athletes, politicians and community leaders — in almost every event I have done. Celebrities add "glitz and glamour" to an event, generating excitement and attracting media. It is usually not too difficult to interest local press and media in talking to a celebrity before and after an event's centerpiece activity. Respected politicians and community leaders always generate good copy for local media through their participation in charity events. It's good for them and good for the event.

I remember one in Chattanooga, Tennessee, hosted by my long time friend Pat Boone. It was for the Bethel Bible School. We brought down 20 Hollywood celebrities to play in a golf-tennis tournament. One of the people on the steering committee for the school was a local sports writer. Every day for two weeks he talked to one of the celebrities coming to Chattanooga and did a piece. There was no way the school could have purchased that amount of newspaper advertising space. It was all for free and it brought out thousands of people who might not otherwise have ever learned of the event.

I do not believe in buying display ads for a fundraising event; I much prefer something called "tradeouts" with a newspaper, billboard company, or radio or TV station. Tradeouts work this way: The media company becomes a sponsor of the event and provides the publicity that brings the event to the public's attention. The charity provides free passes to the event that the media companies give to their best customers as a reward for their continuing loyalty.

Do events grow from year to year? The answer is *yes* if everyone keeps doing what he or she is asked to do. As the word spreads of the success of an event, prices can rise even while attracting more participants. The result is a net increase in dollars generated for the charity. But don't set your financial goals too high in the first year. Find a goal amount that you can attain. If you announce a high number and it is not reached, the inevitable conclusion is a failure. If you raise more than your goal, it looks like a terrific success. One of the best examples of growth was the Michael Landon Celebrity Tennis Tournament that I managed for nine years in Tucson, Arizona. Each year three different nonprofit groups were chosen to benefit from the event. It was a fabulous weekend with a gala/auction on Saturday night between two days of competition attracting 6,000 people on both Saturday and Sunday. Each year the net dollars went up. Through the years people as committed as Michael Landon — William Shatner, Connie Stevens, Lorne Greene, Charlton Heston, Shaquille O'Neal, Willie Shoemaker, and Bruce Jenner — have assisted at various events.

One of the gnawing questions we always face concerns whether a nonprofit with a good name and a great cause, but poor fund raising results, can make a comeback. Our answer will by now sound familiar: *Yes*, if it gets back to the basics with "people who care."

There are four popular sayings that every nonprofit organization needs to take to heart. If these axioms are faithfully adopted, the organization will have a successful event:

- *Charity begins at home.*
- *There is strength in numbers.*
- *Have fun while raising funds.*
- *Together....we can all make a difference.*

Finally, I am often asked to summarize what it takes to have a successful charitable event — one that is both meaningful and memorable, something that people thoroughly enjoy and that earns sufficient money to have made the effort worthwhile. My answer is remarkably simple:

- Organization
- Leadership
- Dedication
- Thoroughness
- Detail
- Follow-through

Provide those attributes and you will have provided a worthwhile event.

I hope that you benefit from this Guide and that your organization is able to apply its points page by page to your event.

CHARITY EVENT PLANNING
Thoughts by Godfrey Harris

CHARITY EVENT PLANNING NOTES

Creating meaningful and memorable charity events always *seems* more daunting than it actually is. If those who plan events follow the hints in these notes and use the forms in this book, they will be surprised at how organized they become and how confident they feel during the planning and implementation process. Best of all, they are likely to enjoy the event itself as much as their guests.

There are three cardinal **RULES** to follow in creating a successful event:

1. **Relax! Don't try to *think* of everything that needs to be done at once. Start by dividing the event into its major components.**
2. **Relax! Don't try to *remember* everything that needs attention. Jot notes as thoughts come to you.**
3. **Relax! Don't try to *accomplish* everything yourself. Let others help by working with you.**

Most planning begins with an idea of what you want to do at the event — raise funds, honor an individual, bring a group together, conduct a ceremony, all of the above. Even though you know where matters stand now and you have the end result in mind, what is missing and what requires planning is resolving the details in between. This might involve selecting:

- VENUES
- INVITATIONS
- DECORATIONS
- REFRESHMENTS
- FAVORS
- ENTERTAINMENT
- SPEAKERS
- AMENITIES.

At each step of the way, remember to be sensitive to the needs of vegetarians, those with food allergies, those in wheelchairs, or those who may be hard of hearing or have trouble seeing.

Event planning, then, is about the creation of a step-by-step process to get you from where you are to where you want to be. If you have a good sense of the resources at your disposal, moving from here to there only needs some orderly thought and reasoned consideration. *The Charity Event Planning Guide* is designed to help. And the starting point is determining the general theme of the event — or the atmosphere you want to generate. Once you have that in mind, obtain fixed commitments for the following crucial elements of any event:

- The best calendar DATE for the event and/or preferred DAY of the week.
- The precise SITE or best LOCATION for the event.
- The attendance of the PRINCIPAL GUEST(s) and/or KEY ATTRACTION(s) for the event.
- The amount you can afford to SPEND on the event.

This book is grounded in a simple philosophy: that PLANNING is as useful and necessary for individuals as it is for government agencies, nonprofit groups, and private businesses. Planning by individuals can prove to be both easy — when using the specially designed forms we have developed and reproduced here — *and* fun — when the planning process follows a logical path from start to finish.

Not all the forms presented in this book will prove useful or necessary to every user for every event; some of the entries may not make sense for a particular situation. That's fine. Nowhere is it written that all of our forms have to be employed or that all spaces on each form have to be completed. Use what you want; forget the rest as you see fit. Remember also that there are no restrictions on making as many copies of the various forms in *The Charity Event Planning Guide* as needed. In fact, since we advise planners to draft and redraft their plans as new circumstances dictate, as new ideas arise, and as collateral decisions are reached, the best planners seem to be the most active with the photocopying equipment. It is a good idea that each time you revise a form, you give each version a consecutive number and the date on which it was written or revised to keep track of the changes.

Another thought. Professional golfers are known to retain the notes they make on every hole on every course they play throughout their careers. Such matters as prevailing winds, distances, sight lines, hole locations, hazards, ridges, slopes and other factors prove invaluable on every subsequent round played on the same course. We recommend that you keep all the forms you make for each event you plan for future reference should you want to repeat or eliminate something or should you want to share your knowledge with others. A title page for these retained forms is on page 64.

You should also know that your event will be a part of any nation's annual activities. In the United States, for example, most people attend some 24 events a year — birthdays, anniversaries, holidays, celebrations, weddings, commemorations, receptions, openings, parties — that someone has carefully planned and prepared. Take the Super Bowl — just one of the 24. Each year more than 100 million Americans gather in homes and halls to watch this annual football game to decide the national professional championship; studies have shown that more than ten million man-hours are devoted to making the arrangements and preparing the food for this event alone.

Finally, realize that the need for advance planning for every undertaking is not shared by everyone. Some refuse to review their assumptions or acknowledge the possibility of change. Others like to do things at the last moment. We think the best events are managed by those with their eyes and ears attuned to everything around them. For instance, we heard of a Senator's aide who recently argued with a Washington, DC travel agent about the need for getting his boss a visa before leaving on a trip to China. "Look," said the aide, "I've been there four times myself and they've always accepted my American Express." The moral of this story is to listen, learn, and then lead. Good planning makes events better.

EVENT ACTIVITIES

FORM A

EVENT ACTIVITIES

Start a separate **EVENT ACTIVITIES FORM** — CEPK FORM A — for each MAJOR ELEMENT of the event — decorations, entertainment, guests, and so forth. The COMPONENTS of each MAJOR ELEMENT are such matters as themes, music, name spellings, and a lot more.

Put ideas, questions, and notes in the THOUGHTS column as they occur to you. Treat your first ideas on each MAJOR ELEMENT as rough notes. For example, you might title one of the sheets INVITATIONS to begin thinking through the details involved in creating and delivering the invitations: Ideas on components such as wording, style and/or material to be used, a printer and/or calligrapher to be located, the amount of time to leave between mailing the invitations and the event itself, and so on.

In the THOUGHTS column alongside each of these COMPONENTS, jot down whatever ideas come to you. Opposite "Wording," for example, you might put reminders of things that need to be decided:

- Should *responses* be handled by phone, EMail, or snail mail? If EMail, what address should be used? If phone, who might be designated to receive the calls?
- Should there be a recommended dress code? How will it be described?
- What time should the event start and end?

The latter two points—occurring in the course of thinking through questions concerning the invitation—are a good example of how each *element* of an event forces consideration about other elements that might have been forgotten or ignored.

EVENT
ACTIVITIES

MAJOR ELEMENT

EVENT
ACTIVITIES

_____/_____/_____ **DATE**

COMPONENTS	THOUGHTS

PHOTOCOPYING ENCOURAGED

CEPG FORM A

PLANNING CALENDARS

FORMS B1 AND B2

PLANNING CALENDARS

Create a **PLANNING CALENDAR** for the period of time between now and the event itself. Use either the **MONTHLY CALENDAR** — CEPK FORM B1 on page 25 — or the **ANNUAL CALENDAR** — CEPK FORM B2 on the next page — to create a schedule of activities that encompasses the scope of your event.

Enter the appropriate date against each day in the month on CEPK FORM B1 or the dates of the Mondays to Fridays for each week of the month on CEPK FORM B2. When a month has say five Mondays or five Thursdays, instead of the normal four, draw a diagonal line through the box from the northeast corner to the southwest corner to accommodate all the days in a full month.

In filling in the boxes, it is sometimes easier to put ending dates for each activity first and work back to the starting date (e.g., the date invitations are to be mailed, the date the invitation master is to be delivered to the printer, the date the wording needs to be approved, and so on.)

MONTHLY CALENDAR

MONTH

VERSION #_____

MONTHLY CALENDAR

_____/_____/_____ **DATE**

SUNDAY		MONDAY		TUESDAY		WEDNESDAY	THURSDAY	FRIDAY		SATURDAY	
SUNDAY		MONDAY		TUESDAY		WEDNESDAY	THURSDAY	FRIDAY		SATURDAY	
SUNDAY		MONDAY		TUESDAY		WEDNESDAY	THURSDAY	FRIDAY		SATURDAY	
SUNDAY		MONDAY		TUESDAY		WEDNESDAY	THURSDAY	FRIDAY		SATURDAY	
SUNDAY		MONDAY		TUESDAY		WEDNESDAY	THURSDAY	FRIDAY		SATURDAY	

PHOTOCOPYING ENCOURAGED

CEPG **FORM B1**

ANNUAL CALENDAR

VERSION #____

	YEAR

ANNUAL CALENDAR

	JAN	FEB	MAR	APR	MAY	JUN	JUL	AUG	SEP	OCT	NOV	DEC
WEEK 1	___TO___	___TO___	___TO___	___TO___	___TO___	___TO___	___TO___	___TO___	___TO___	___TO___	___TO___	___TO___
WEEK 2	___TO___	___TO___	___TO___	___TO___	___TO___	___TO___	___TO___	___TO___	___TO___	___TO___	___TO___	___TO___
WEEK 3	___TO___	___TO___	___TO___	___TO___	___TO___	___TO___	___TO___	___TO___	___TO___	___TO___	___TO___	___TO___
WEEK 4	___TO___	___TO___	___TO___	___TO___	___TO___	___TO___	___TO___	___TO___	___TO___	___TO___	___TO___	___TO___
WEEK 5	___TO___	___TO___	___TO___	___TO___	___TO___	___TO___	___TO___	___TO___	___TO___	___TO___	___TO___	___TO___

PHOTOCOPYING ENCOURAGED

CEPG FORM B2

FUND RAISING AND SPONSORSHIPS

FORM C

FUND RAISING AND SPONSORSHIPS

If you need financial support for an event, the most likely sources of help are those closest to you. Start with family, friends, and associates. Ask them to contribute to or invest in your project, but only for an amount that they truly wouldn't miss or have no immediate need for. On your own or with others, move outward to reach those individuals or organizations with an affiliation to or affinity for the event itself.

Be realistic. Donations or contributions are usually made to support events when the *giver* can justify two values in terms of the cost involved:

- The benefit to the recipient getting the money; and

- The benefit to the donor providing the money.

Keep both factors in mind when you rehearse your oral pitch or draft your written proposal. Make sure to cover the purpose of the event; its importance to the community; its special features; the people, organizations, and/or institutions involved; how benefactors will receive credit for their participation; and the basis for your belief in the event's ultimate success. Make your pitch or your document something easily repeated or copied for those who will have to forward your request to others for approval.

FUND RAISING

FUND
RAISING

IDENTIFY ELEMENT FOR SPONSORSHIP OR WHOLE EVENT

VERSION #_____

_____/_____/_____ **DATE**

CONTACT THIS PERSON	TO REACH THIS POTENTIAL SOURCE	FOR THIS TYPE OF DONATION		FOR THIS PERCEIVED BENEFIT
		ITEM	$	
		ITEM	$	
		ITEM	$	
		ITEM	$	
		ITEM	$	
		ITEM	$	
		ITEM	$	
		ITEM	$	
		ITEM	$	
		ITEM	$	
		ITEM	$	
		ITEM	$	

PHOTOCOPYING ENCOURAGED

CEPG FORM C

LAYOUT MAP

FORM D

LAYOUT MAP

Create a "blueprint" of the venue(s) to be used for your event on the **LAYOUT MAP** — CEPK FORM D. If you need more space, combine several blank forms together or expand the form on a photocopying machine. Determine the actual size and shape of the venue(s) where the principal activities will take place.

The grid on CEPK FORM D consists of 15 horizontal and 10 vertical squares. Draw a rough outline around the squares in the shape of the space you will use. Let each square represent an actual on-the-ground measurement (each representing so many feet or meters) to allow you to get an approximate idea of how everything will be arranged and spaced.

Trace or cutout as many shapes as needed from CEPK FORM E to make trial arrangements of the tables, chairs, and ancillary equipment. Remember that you are working with estimated size and distances; precise placements will have to wait until you are on the ground. Be sure to leave sufficient room for the movement of people (including those in wheelchairs, with walkers, or needing other forms of assistance) and plan sites for such traditional aspects of an event as a registration desk, podium, refreshment center, back-of-the-room sales area, and so on. If more than one room or space is involved in an event, make as many duplicates of the Layout Map as needed.

LAYOUT
MAP

LAYOUT
MAP

VERSION #_____

_____/_____/_____ **DATE**

PHOTOCOPYING ENCOURAGED

CEPK FORM D

FURNISHINGS

FORM E

FURNISHINGS

Trace or cut out the table shape(s), seating pattern(s), and ancillary equipment — CEPK FORM E — needed to handle guests, presentations, and/or serving areas.

If your event involves rows of seats arranged in auditorium style, determine the allowable number in each row as well as the proper width of the aisle(s) from the venue manager and/or the fire department before creating any seating blocs. Remember that it is infinitely easier to be in compliance with all the rules and fulfill all the needs of an event when you move and adjust furniture and equipment *on paper* rather than having to shift the actual furniture and equipment on the ground.

Here are some standard sizes and typical spacings to help you plan your event:

- Seats: 16" (40cm) wide. In auditorium seating, leave 18" (46cm) between the back of the seat in one row and the front of the seat in the next row.
- Tables: 72" (183cm) in diameter for 12 people; 60" (152cm) for 10 people; 52" (132cm) for 8 people; 48" (122cm) for 6 people; and 36" (92cm) for 4 people.
- Aisle widths or table spacing: 36" (92cm) between the edges of objects.

Remember, too, that we are operating in the 21st century. Make sure your event has wi-fi connectivity and all the technological necessities to assure good attendance. Mark the power outlets and wi-fi hotspots on your facility maps. Print or post user names and/or passwords that activate Internet connections.

FURNISHINGS

TABLE
SIZES/SHAPES

(10)

(8)

(4)

(2)

SCREEN

OVERHEAD

MICROPHONES

LIGHTS

LECTURN

SPEAKERS

HEATERS

FANS

COAT RACKS

EASELS

PLANTS

(4)

(6)

(8)

AISLES

AUDITORIUM SEATING
CONFIGURATIONS

PHOTOCOPYING ENCOURAGEDC

EPK FORM E

THE CHARITY
EVENT
PLANNING GUIDE

EVENT BUDGET

FORM F

EVENT BUDGET

Building an **EVENT BUDGET** — CEPK FORM F — is like constructing a house — every aspect of the construction from the concrete in the foundation to the shingles on the roof have a specific cost with the value of each dependent on both the quality and the quantity involved.

Just as an architect sketches out a concept before continually refining the elements into an affordable and pleasing structure, so those who plan events need to work from an overall vision of the event before trying to find the right balance of design and ingredients to insure both affordability and memorability.

When costs are not known, make your best guess and refine them as additional information becomes available.

EVENT BUDGET

VERSION #_____

IDENTIFY MAJOR ELEMENT OR WHOLE EVENT

EVENT BUDGET

_____/_____/_____ **DATE**

THIS ACTIVITY	WITH THESE COMPONENTS	AT THIS UNIT COST		THIS NUMBER OF UNITS		THIS TOTAL AMOUNT
			X		=	$
			X		=	$
			X		=	$
			X		=	$
			X		=	$
			X		=	$
			X		=	$
			X		=	$
			X		=	$
			X		=	$
			X		=	$
		TOTAL			=	$

PHOTOCOPYING ENCOURAGED

CEPK FORM F

THE CHARITY
EVENT
PLANNING GUIDE

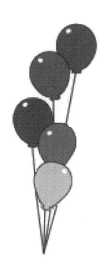

PLANNING GUIDE

FORM G

PLANNING GUIDE

Because the **PLANNING CALENDAR** — CEPK FORM B —can become too cluttered, start building a **PLANNING GUIDE.** It allows you to record the smallest detail that must be accomplished along with the date and / or time of its expected completion, its cost, and the person charged with accomplishing it.

As you work through this form, you may have to go back to change dates already entered on the **PLANNING CALENDAR.** For example, you may have allowed two weeks to address the invitations. Working backwards, you may find that the date inadvertently selected to pick up the invitations is the Friday start of a three-day holiday when traffic may be heavy or the print shop may close early. As a result, you would want to add a few days to this part of the schedule. The more refined your thinking becomes to deal with challenges and the unexpected, the more organized you will be and the more relaxed you will feel.

PLANNING GUIDE

VERSION #_____

IDENTIFY COMPONENT

PLANNING GUIDE

_____/_____/_____ DATE

ACCOMPLISH THIS TASK	WITH THIS PERSON'S HELP	BY THIS DATE/TIME	AT THIS COST	DONE?

PHOTOCOPYING ENCOURAGED

CEPK FORM G

THE CHARITY
EVENT
PLANNING GUIDE

EVENT CHECKLIST

FORM H

EVENT CHECKLIST

All the activities that must come together on the day of the event itself — from flower delivery to catering to transporting the principals — should be listed on the **EVENT CHECKLIST** — CEPK FORM H — along with the name of persons responsible for seeing that the items or individuals get to the event site from their pre-event location.

EVENT CHECKLIST

VERSION #_____

IDENTIFY SEPARATE ELEMENTS OF EVENT

EVENT CHECKLIST

_____/_____/_____ **DATE**

√	ITEM	LOCATION	RESPONSIBILITY	√	ITEM	LOCATION	RESPONSIBILITY

PHOTOCOPYING ENCOURAGED

CEPK **FORM H**

THE CHARITY
EVENT
PLANNING GUIDE

EVENT PROGRAM

FORM I

EVENT PROGRAM

Every activity that is planned for the event itself should be noted on the **EVENT PRO-GRAM** — EPK FORM I — to ensure that the entire effort runs smoothly.

This form should be used and refined after rehearsals or following a verbal "walk through" of the event with other participants. Don't guess. Time each activity with a watch and make sure to leave mandatory catch-up periods for unavoidable delays and unexpected occurrences.

Rehearse every aspect of the program. Think through who should make announcements and when they should be made. Check sound levels to make sure conversations are not overwhelmed by a band, DJ, or adjacent activities.

EVENT
PROGRAM

VERSION #____

EVENT TITLE

EVENT
PROGRAM

____/____/____ DATE

AT THIS TIME	THIS ACTIVITY OCCURS	INVOLVING THIS DETAIL
____:____ __M		
____:____ __M		
____:____ __M		
____:____ __M		
____:____ __M		
____:____ __M		
____:____ __M		
____:____ __M		
____:____ __M		
____:____ __M		
____:____ __M		
____:____ __M		
____:____ __M		
____:____ __M		
____:____ __M		
____:____ __M		
____:____ __M		
____:____ __M		
____:____ __M		

PHOTOCOPYING ENCOURAGED

CEPK FORM I

THE CHARITY
EVENT
PLANNING GUIDE

CONTINGENCY CONSIDERATIONS

FORM J

CONTINGENCY CONSIDERATIONS

List the possible and potential problems that might befall a principal, the type of adverse weather that might occur for the area or season of the event, and the type of emergencies that have happened in the recent past on **CONTINGENCY CONSIDERATIONS** — CEPK FORM J.

For each contingency listed, note what action might be taken to ameliorate a situation and how that action might affect the site, the timing, and / or the guests. Consider the possibility of a thunder storm, freeway closure, police emergency, etc.

You need not be precise in your descriptions or your potential adjustment to a perceived problem. It is enough at this stage to consider a few options or maneuvers that might be employed should a problem actually occur. As a particular contingency becomes more imminent, you can refine your adjustments and / or solutions.

We would amend an old Massachusetts Mutual Insurance Company slogan this way: *You can't predict, but you can prepare.*

CONTINGENCY CONSIDERATIONS

VERSION #_____

EVENT TITLE

_____/_____/_____ DATE

TYPE OF CONCERN	IF THIS OCCURS... (DESCRIBE BRIEFLY)	POSSIBLE CHANGES IN SITE/TIMING	POTENTIAL IMPACT ON GUESTS
PROBLEM BEFALLING A PRINCIPAL			
ECONOMIC/FINANCIAL COMPLICATIONS			
WEATHER FACTORS			
POTENTIAL NATURAL DISASTER			
ACCIDENT OR OTHER EMERGENCY OCCURENCE			
POLICE/LABOR ACTIONS			

PHOTOCOPYING ENCOURAGED

CEPK FORM J

EVENT GOAL AND EVALUATION

FORMS K1 AND K2

EVENT GOAL AND EVALUATION

We see planning a little differently than others. We believe that the goal statement—CEPK FORM K—should be formalized only *after* all the planning steps have been contemplated and the major arrangements have been considered.

We believe this makes the goal statement much more realistic, encouraging organizers to review plans and arrangements to insure that they meet their intended target. Political observers have come to realize that the political continuum from radical to reactionary is circular rather than linear (with little *real* difference between these two seeming extremes). By the same token, planning an event can end with the initial goals being re-articulated and refined at the conclusion of the process.

We also believe that you should evaluate an event immediately after it ends. Gather everyone's comments, as well as your own, for a hard-nosed assessment of what went right, what went wrong, and why. Don't wait. If you delay any length of time to review a just concluded event, you are likely to lose key details and perhaps be condemned to make the same mistakes again.

Justice Oliver Wendell Holmes, Jr., once famously noted that there is no good writing, only good *re-writing*. As a result, it isn't how you draft your original **EVENT GOAL** or your preliminary **EVALUATION** on CEPK FORMS K1 AND K2 that counts, it's how close the final version comes to expressing what will make an event a success and what will make another similar event an even more impressive success in the future.

EVENT
GOAL

EVENT TITLE

EVENT
GOAL

TO...

PHOTOCOPYING ENCOURAGED

CEPK FORM K1

EVALUATION

ACTIVITY

EVALUATION

VERSION_____

____/____/____ DATE

THIS ASPECT	COULD HAVE BEEN IMPROVED BY	WITH ATTENTION TO THIS DETAIL

PHOTOCOPYING ENCOURAGED

CEPK FORM K2

SAMPLE COMPLETED FORMS

EVENT ACTIVITIES

MEETING ROOM
MAJOR ELEMENT

VERSION _1_
05/11/01 DATE

COMPONENTS	THOUGHTS
REFRESHMENTS	COFFEE / TEA / COKE / DIET COKE / COOKIES ↳ ENG. BREAKFAST / HERBAL DIET 7-UP
ROOM	U-SHAPED TABLE / DETACHED HEAD TABLE - BOOK SALE AREA
EQUIPMENT	OVERHEAD / EASLE OR CHALK BOARD / PORTABLE (LAPEL) MIKE
NAME PLAQUES	DO WE WANT? WHO WRITES NAMES? FIRST ONLY OR BOTH?

EPK FORM A

EVENT BUDGET

WOM SEMINAR
IDENTIFY MAJOR ELEMENT OR WHOLE EVENT

VERSION _2_
06/11/01 DATE

THIS ACTIVITY...	WITH THESE COMPONENTS...	AT THIS UNIT COST...	X	THIS NUMBER OF UNITS...	=	THIS TOTAL AMOUNT...
MAILINGS	LETTERS	$.65/PC	X	1000 PIECES	=	$650
	POSTCARDS	$.33/PC	X	1000 PIECES	=	$330
ADVERTISING	LA TIMES	$290/INCH	X	2 INSERTIONS	=	$580
	DAILY NEWS	$190/INCH	X	3 INSERTIONS	=	$570
MATERIALS	MANUAL	$2.25 EA	X	50 COPIES	=	$113
	CERTIFICATES	$1.00 EA	X	50	=	$50
	PRIZES	$1.00 EA	X	15 TICKETS	=	$15
HOTEL	ROOM	$100/HR	X	3 HOURS	=	$300
	REFRESH.	$1.50/HEAD	X	50	=	$75
	PARKING	$3.00/CAR	X	20 CARS	=	$60
CONTING.		12% OF SUB-TOTAL (↑)	X	[$2473]	=	$297
				TOTAL	=	$2770

EPK FORM F

PLANNING CALENDAR

JULY
MONTH

VERSION _3_
05/15/01 DATE

SUNDAY	MONDAY	TUESDAY	WEDNESDAY	THURSDAY	FRIDAY	SATURDAY
1 RUN FINAL NEWSPAPER AD	2	3	4	5 MAIL SECOND POSTCARD TO LIST	6	7
8	9	10	11	12 MAKE REMINDER CALLS	13 MAKE REMINDER CALLS	14
15	16 CLOSE SEMINAR CREATE ROSTER	17 BOX MATERIALS	18 TAKE MATERIALS TO HOTEL	19 SEMINAR	20 CLEAN UP	21
22	23 ASSESS-MENT LETTERS OUT	24	25	26	27	28
29	30	31				

EPK FORM B

EVENT PROGRAM

WOM SEMINAR
EVENT TITLE

VERSION _3_
06/17/01 DATE

AT THIS TIME...	THIS ACTIVITY OCCURS...	UNDER THESE CONDITIONS...
12:00	DESIREE @ HOTEL	GETS ROOM OPEN
	PENNY @ HOTEL	SETS UP BOOK SALE
	JEFF @ HOME CHANGING	
1:00	JEFF ARRANGES SAMPLES / OVERHEADS / PRIZES	AT HOTEL
2:00	SEMINAR BEGINS	JEFF
3:15	BREAK TIME	BARBARA HOSTS
4:30	SEMINAR ENDS	CERTS AWARDED
5:00	DEPART HOTEL	ROOM CLOSED

EPK FORM I

EVENT DESIGNATION

EVENT DATE

THE CHARITY
EVENT
PLANNING GUIDE

NOTES/IDEAS/CONCERNS

INDEX

DAVID MIRISCH is the president of David Mirisch Enterprises, an international event production company that also places Hollywood celebrities and world-class athletes in paid and non-paid personal appearances.

His company has produced more than 2,500 fundraising events throughout the United States and in 7 foreign countries including Canada, Bahamas, Ecuador, Haiti, Mexico, Japan, and Malaysia. The events have involved recreational activities such as golf, tennis, softball, bowling, walks, fishing, skiing, and equestrian demonstrations as well as social events such as fashion shows, luncheons, casino parties, and over 500 Galas/Auctions.

David Mirisch has personally helped nonprofits raise more than $35,000,000 during his 40+ year career. Depending on the event and the organization's goals, some have sought as little as $10,000 while others have generated more than $1,000,000. Mirisch brings his knowledge of social habits and his vast experience to help organizations put on great events that raise as many dollars as possible.

David is a member of the renowned Mirisch family, a legendary power in the motion picture industry. Members of the family have produced 72 feature films, won 24 Academy Awards — including a remarkable *three* "Best Picture of the Year" Oscars for *West Side Story*, *The Apartment*, and *Heat of the Night*. Prior to becoming involved in fund-raising for the nonprofit world, Mirisch was a publicity field agent for United Artists before opening his own public relations agency. That agency represented such Hollywood luminaries as Merv Griffin, Johnny Mathis, Pat Boone, Perry Como, Raquel Welch, Lindsay Wagner and Wilt Chamberlain. David is also credited with having discovered Farrah Fawcett in 1968.

David is married and now lives in Missoula, Montana.

GODFREY HARRIS has been a public policy consultant based in Los Angeles, California, since 1968. He began consulting after serving as a university instructor at UCLA and Rutgers, a U.S. Army intelligence officer, a U.S. foreign service officer with the Department of State, an organizational specialist in President Lyndon Johnson's Executive Office, and as a program manager for an international financial company in Geneva.

In all of these positions, Harris honed his planning skills when he was called upon to organize or manage meetings, dinners, trips, exhibits, funerals, conferences, seminars, receptions, parties, and other diplomatic, social, and commercial events requiring coordinating the activities of colleagues, contractors, and guests. At present, he serves as Curator of the Da Vinci Exhibit, a museum-quality display of the machines, art, and philosophy of Leonardo da Vinci.

As President of Harris/Ragan Management Group, Harris has focused the firm's activities on projects that offer alternative solutions to matters of community concern. In fulfilling that role, he has specialized in political and economic analysis; marketing public and private sector services through word of mouth advertising; developing new environmental and commercial products; promoting international tourism to various destinations; and creating commemorative, enlightening, and educational events.

Harris has written on his own or with associates 63 other books on business and public policy topics. He holds degrees from Stanford University and the University of California, Los Angeles, and is listed in Who's Who in America and Who's Who in the World.